50 The Big Book of Healthy Sweets Recipes

By: Kelly Johnson

Table of Contents

- Almond Flour Chocolate Chip Cookies
- Avocado Chocolate Mousse
- Coconut Macaroons
- Banana Oatmeal Cookies
- Greek Yogurt Parfait with Fresh Berries
- Raw Date and Nut Energy Balls
- Chia Seed Pudding with Mango
- Baked Apple Cinnamon Chips
- Dark Chocolate Almond Bark
- Healthy Apple Crisp
- Zucchini Brownies
- Coconut-Lime Bliss Balls
- Protein-Packed Peanut Butter Cups
- Almond Joy Energy Bites
- Cashew Butter Chocolate Truffles
- Baked Banana Donuts
- Healthy Carrot Cake with Almond Flour
- Oatmeal Raisin Cookies
- Frozen Yogurt Bark with Fruit
- Dark Chocolate-Covered Strawberries
- Paleo Pumpkin Pie
- Healthy Lemon Bars
- Blueberry Almond Muffins
- Choco-Peanut Butter Smoothie
- Coconut Chia Energy Bites
- Vegan Chocolate Chip Cookies
- Caramelized Pineapple with Cinnamon
- Baked Oatmeal Cups with Berries
- Healthy Cheesecake Bites
- Sweet Potato Brownies
- Coconut Milk Panna Cotta
- Strawberry Almond Cake
- Matcha Energy Bars
- Maple Cinnamon Roasted Nuts
- Date-Sweetened Brownies

- Apple Almond Crumble
- Healthy Chocolate Coconut Cupcakes
- Chia Jam on Almond Crackers
- Vegan Lemon Coconut Truffles
- Banana Chia Pudding
- Almond Butter Banana Ice Cream
- Avocado Lime Cheesecake
- Chocolate-Peanut Butter Protein Balls
- Pumpkin Energy Bars
- Raw Chocolate Coconut Fudge
- Oat and Honey Granola Bars
- Strawberry Coconut Sorbet
- Cinnamon Pecan Bites
- Mango-Coconut Popsicles
- Almond Flour Chocolate Cake

Almond Flour Chocolate Chip Cookies

Ingredients

- 2 cups almond flour
- 1/2 tsp baking soda
- 1/4 tsp salt
- 1/4 cup coconut oil, melted
- 1/4 cup maple syrup or honey
- 1 tsp vanilla extract
- 1/2 cup dark chocolate chips (gluten-free)
- 1 egg (or flax egg for vegan option)

Instructions

1. **Preheat the Oven:**
    - Preheat your oven to 350°F (175°C). Line a baking sheet with parchment paper.
2. **Mix the Dry Ingredients:**
    - In a medium bowl, combine the almond flour, baking soda, and salt.
3. **Combine the Wet Ingredients:**
    - In a separate bowl, whisk together the melted coconut oil, maple syrup, vanilla extract, and egg until smooth.
4. **Combine the Mixtures:**
    - Add the wet ingredients to the dry ingredients and stir until combined. Fold in the chocolate chips.
5. **Shape and Bake:**
    - Scoop spoonfuls of dough and roll them into balls. Place them on the prepared baking sheet and gently flatten each cookie. Bake for 10-12 minutes until golden brown around the edges.
6. **Cool:**
    - Allow the cookies to cool on the baking sheet for a few minutes before transferring them to a wire rack to cool completely.

Avocado Chocolate Mousse

Ingredients

- 2 ripe avocados, peeled and pitted
- 1/4 cup unsweetened cocoa powder
- 1/4 cup maple syrup or honey
- 1 tsp vanilla extract
- 1/4 cup coconut milk (or any non-dairy milk)
- A pinch of salt
- 2 tbsp dark chocolate chips (optional, for garnish)

Instructions

1. **Blend the Ingredients:**
    - In a blender or food processor, combine the avocados, cocoa powder, maple syrup, vanilla extract, coconut milk, and salt. Blend until smooth and creamy.
2. **Chill:**
    - Transfer the mousse into serving dishes and refrigerate for at least 30 minutes to allow the flavors to meld.
3. **Serve:**
    - Garnish with chocolate chips or fresh berries and enjoy!

Coconut Macaroons

Ingredients

- 2 cups shredded unsweetened coconut
- 1/4 cup honey or maple syrup
- 2 egg whites
- 1 tsp vanilla extract
- A pinch of salt

Instructions

1. **Preheat the Oven:**
    - Preheat the oven to 325°F (165°C). Line a baking sheet with parchment paper.
2. **Mix the Ingredients:**
    - In a medium bowl, combine the shredded coconut, honey or maple syrup, egg whites, vanilla extract, and salt.
3. **Form the Macaroons:**
    - Use a spoon to scoop out the mixture and form small mounds on the baking sheet.
4. **Bake:**
    - Bake for 15-18 minutes, or until the macaroons are golden brown around the edges.
5. **Cool:**
    - Let the macaroons cool on the baking sheet for a few minutes before transferring to a wire rack to cool completely.

Banana Oatmeal Cookies

Ingredients

- 2 ripe bananas, mashed
- 1 1/2 cups rolled oats
- 1/4 cup almond butter or peanut butter
- 1/4 cup dark chocolate chips or raisins (optional)
- 1/2 tsp cinnamon
- 1/4 tsp vanilla extract
- 1/4 tsp salt

Instructions

1. **Preheat the Oven:**
   - Preheat the oven to 350°F (175°C). Line a baking sheet with parchment paper.
2. **Mix the Ingredients:**
   - In a large bowl, mash the bananas. Stir in the oats, almond butter, chocolate chips (or raisins), cinnamon, vanilla extract, and salt.
3. **Shape the Cookies:**
   - Scoop spoonfuls of the mixture and form small mounds on the baking sheet. Flatten slightly with the back of a spoon.
4. **Bake:**
   - Bake for 10-12 minutes, or until golden brown.
5. **Cool:**
   - Let the cookies cool on the baking sheet for a few minutes before transferring them to a wire rack to cool completely.

Greek Yogurt Parfait with Fresh Berries

Ingredients

- 1 cup Greek yogurt (plain or vanilla)
- 1/2 cup mixed fresh berries (strawberries, blueberries, raspberries)
- 2 tbsp honey or maple syrup
- 1/4 cup granola or nuts (optional)

Instructions

1. **Assemble the Parfait:**
     - In a glass or bowl, layer the Greek yogurt, fresh berries, and granola or nuts (if using).
2. **Add Sweetener:**
     - Drizzle honey or maple syrup over the top for sweetness.
3. **Serve:**
     - Serve immediately or refrigerate for later.

Raw Date and Nut Energy Balls

Ingredients

- 1 cup pitted dates
- 1/2 cup raw almonds or cashews
- 1/4 cup shredded coconut
- 1 tbsp chia seeds (optional)
- 1 tsp vanilla extract
- A pinch of sea salt

Instructions

1. **Process the Ingredients:**
    - In a food processor, combine the dates, almonds (or cashews), coconut, chia seeds (if using), vanilla extract, and salt. Pulse until the mixture is sticky and starts to come together.
2. **Form the Balls:**
    - Scoop out the mixture and roll it into small balls.
3. **Chill:**
    - Place the energy balls on a tray lined with parchment paper and refrigerate for at least 30 minutes before serving.

Chia Seed Pudding with Mango

Ingredients

- 1/4 cup chia seeds
- 1 cup coconut milk (or any non-dairy milk)
- 1 tbsp honey or maple syrup
- 1/2 tsp vanilla extract
- 1/2 cup diced fresh mango

Instructions

1. **Make the Pudding:**
   - In a bowl, combine the chia seeds, coconut milk, honey, and vanilla extract. Stir well, then cover and refrigerate for at least 4 hours or overnight.
2. **Serve:**
   - Before serving, top with fresh diced mango.

Baked Apple Cinnamon Chips

Ingredients

- 2 large apples, thinly sliced
- 1 tsp ground cinnamon
- 1 tbsp coconut sugar (optional)

Instructions

1. **Preheat the Oven:**
    - Preheat your oven to 200°F (90°C). Line a baking sheet with parchment paper.
2. **Prepare the Apples:**
    - Core and slice the apples into very thin rounds. Place them on the baking sheet in a single layer.
3. **Season:**
    - Sprinkle the apple slices with cinnamon and coconut sugar (if using).
4. **Bake:**
    - Bake for 1.5 to 2 hours, flipping halfway through, until the apple slices are crisp and golden.
5. **Cool:**
    - Allow the chips to cool completely before serving.

Dark Chocolate Almond Bark

Ingredients

- 2 cups dark chocolate (70% cocoa or higher)
- 1/2 cup raw almonds, chopped
- 1/4 tsp sea salt
- 1 tsp vanilla extract

Instructions

1. **Melt the Chocolate:**
   - In a microwave-safe bowl, melt the dark chocolate in 20-second intervals, stirring in between, until smooth.
2. **Add Vanilla and Salt:**
   - Stir in the vanilla extract and sea salt into the melted chocolate.
3. **Add Almonds:**
   - Stir in the chopped almonds until evenly distributed.
4. **Spread and Chill:**
   - Pour the chocolate mixture onto a parchment-lined baking sheet and spread it out into a thin, even layer.
5. **Set:**
   - Place the bark in the fridge to set for about 30 minutes, or until completely firm.
6. **Break and Serve:**
   - Once set, break the bark into pieces and enjoy!

Healthy Apple Crisp

Ingredients

- 4 medium apples, peeled and sliced
- 1 tbsp lemon juice
- 1/2 cup rolled oats
- 1/4 cup almond flour
- 1/4 cup chopped walnuts or pecans
- 1/4 cup honey or maple syrup
- 1 tsp cinnamon
- 1/4 tsp nutmeg
- 2 tbsp coconut oil, melted
- Pinch of salt

Instructions

1. **Preheat the Oven:**
    - Preheat your oven to 350°F (175°C).
2. **Prepare the Apples:**
    - In a large bowl, toss the sliced apples with lemon juice. Spread the apples in a greased 9x9 baking dish.
3. **Make the Topping:**
    - In a bowl, combine the oats, almond flour, walnuts, cinnamon, nutmeg, honey, coconut oil, and salt. Stir until everything is evenly combined.
4. **Assemble and Bake:**
    - Sprinkle the topping evenly over the apples. Bake for 35-40 minutes or until the topping is golden and the apples are tender.
5. **Serve:**
    - Serve warm on its own or with a scoop of Greek yogurt or vanilla ice cream.

Zucchini Brownies

Ingredients

- 1 1/2 cups zucchini, grated (about 2 medium zucchinis)
- 1/2 cup almond flour
- 1/4 cup cocoa powder
- 1/2 tsp baking soda
- 1/4 tsp salt
- 1/2 cup maple syrup or honey
- 2 eggs
- 1/4 cup almond butter or peanut butter
- 1 tsp vanilla extract
- 1/4 cup dark chocolate chips (optional)

Instructions

1. **Preheat the Oven:**
   - Preheat your oven to 350°F (175°C). Grease an 8x8-inch baking pan.
2. **Prepare the Zucchini:**
   - Grate the zucchini and squeeze out the excess moisture using a clean towel or paper towel.
3. **Mix the Dry Ingredients:**
   - In a bowl, whisk together almond flour, cocoa powder, baking soda, and salt.
4. **Mix the Wet Ingredients:**
   - In another bowl, whisk together maple syrup, eggs, almond butter, and vanilla extract.
5. **Combine and Bake:**
   - Add the wet ingredients to the dry ingredients and stir in the grated zucchini. Fold in the chocolate chips if using. Pour the batter into the prepared pan and bake for 25-30 minutes.
6. **Cool and Serve:**
   - Allow the brownies to cool completely before cutting into squares and serving.

Coconut-Lime Bliss Balls

Ingredients

- 1 cup unsweetened shredded coconut
- 1/2 cup cashew nuts
- 2 tbsp honey or maple syrup
- Zest of 1 lime
- 1 tbsp lime juice
- 1/2 tsp vanilla extract
- Pinch of salt

Instructions

1. **Process the Ingredients:**
   - In a food processor, combine the shredded coconut, cashews, honey, lime zest, lime juice, vanilla extract, and salt. Process until the mixture is sticky and well combined.
2. **Shape the Balls:**
   - Roll the mixture into small balls using your hands, about 1-inch in diameter.
3. **Chill:**
   - Place the balls on a parchment-lined tray and refrigerate for at least 30 minutes before serving.

Protein-Packed Peanut Butter Cups

Ingredients

- 1/2 cup peanut butter (natural, unsweetened)
- 1/4 cup protein powder (vanilla or chocolate)
- 2 tbsp coconut flour
- 2 tbsp honey or maple syrup
- 1/4 tsp vanilla extract
- 3/4 cup dark chocolate chips (for the coating)

Instructions

1. **Prepare the Filling:**
   - In a bowl, combine the peanut butter, protein powder, coconut flour, honey, and vanilla extract. Mix until smooth and well combined.
2. **Form the Cups:**
   - Line a mini muffin tin with paper liners. Spoon a small amount of the peanut butter mixture into each cup, pressing down to form a flat layer.
3. **Melt the Chocolate:**
   - Melt the dark chocolate chips in the microwave, stirring every 20 seconds until smooth.
4. **Assemble:**
   - Spoon a layer of melted chocolate over the peanut butter filling, covering it completely.
5. **Chill:**
   - Refrigerate for at least 30 minutes until the cups are set.

Almond Joy Energy Bites

Ingredients

- 1 cup rolled oats
- 1/4 cup almond butter
- 1/4 cup unsweetened shredded coconut
- 1/4 cup dark chocolate chips
- 1/4 cup raw almonds
- 2 tbsp honey or maple syrup
- 1/2 tsp vanilla extract

Instructions

1. **Mix the Ingredients:**
    - In a bowl, combine all of the ingredients. Stir well to combine until the mixture sticks together.
2. **Form the Bites:**
    - Roll the mixture into small balls, about 1-inch in diameter.
3. **Chill:**
    - Refrigerate the energy bites for at least 30 minutes before serving.

Cashew Butter Chocolate Truffles

Ingredients

- 1/2 cup cashew butter
- 1/4 cup dark chocolate chips
- 2 tbsp honey or maple syrup
- 1/2 tsp vanilla extract
- 1/4 cup unsweetened cocoa powder (for coating)

Instructions

1. **Prepare the Truffle Mixture:**
   - In a bowl, combine cashew butter, honey, and vanilla extract. Melt the chocolate chips and stir them into the mixture until smooth.
2. **Form the Truffles:**
   - Scoop the mixture into small portions and roll into balls.
3. **Coat the Truffles:**
   - Roll each truffle in cocoa powder to coat it.
4. **Chill:**
   - Place the truffles on a parchment-lined tray and refrigerate for at least 30 minutes before serving.

Baked Banana Donuts

Ingredients

- 1 cup oat flour
- 1/2 tsp baking powder
- 1/4 tsp cinnamon
- 1/4 tsp salt
- 1 ripe banana, mashed
- 1 egg
- 1/4 cup almond milk
- 2 tbsp honey or maple syrup
- 1/2 tsp vanilla extract

Instructions

1. **Preheat the Oven:**
   - Preheat your oven to 350°F (175°C). Grease a donut pan.
2. **Mix the Dry Ingredients:**
   - In a bowl, combine the oat flour, baking powder, cinnamon, and salt.
3. **Mix the Wet Ingredients:**
   - In another bowl, whisk together the mashed banana, egg, almond milk, honey, and vanilla extract.
4. **Combine and Bake:**
   - Add the wet ingredients to the dry ingredients and stir until well combined. Spoon the batter into the donut pan.
5. **Bake:**
   - Bake for 12-15 minutes or until a toothpick comes out clean. Allow to cool slightly before removing from the pan.

Healthy Carrot Cake with Almond Flour

Ingredients

- 2 cups almond flour
- 1/2 cup shredded coconut
- 2 tsp baking powder
- 1/2 tsp cinnamon
- 1/4 tsp nutmeg
- 1/4 tsp salt
- 3 large eggs
- 1/4 cup honey or maple syrup
- 1/4 cup coconut oil, melted
- 1 tsp vanilla extract
- 1 1/2 cups shredded carrots
- 1/4 cup chopped walnuts (optional)

Instructions

1. **Preheat the Oven:**
   - Preheat your oven to 350°F (175°C) and grease a 9-inch round cake pan.
2. **Mix the Dry Ingredients:**
   - In a bowl, whisk together almond flour, shredded coconut, baking powder, cinnamon, nutmeg, and salt.
3. **Mix the Wet Ingredients:**
   - In another bowl, whisk together eggs, honey or maple syrup, coconut oil, and vanilla extract.
4. **Combine and Add Carrots:**
   - Add the wet ingredients to the dry ingredients and mix until combined. Fold in the shredded carrots and walnuts (if using).
5. **Bake:**
   - Pour the batter into the prepared cake pan and bake for 25-30 minutes, or until a toothpick comes out clean.
6. **Cool and Serve:**
   - Allow the cake to cool before serving.

Oatmeal Raisin Cookies

Ingredients

- 1 1/2 cups rolled oats
- 1/2 cup almond flour
- 1/2 tsp baking soda
- 1/2 tsp cinnamon
- 1/4 tsp salt
- 1/2 cup coconut oil, melted
- 1/4 cup maple syrup
- 1 large egg
- 1 tsp vanilla extract
- 1/2 cup raisins

Instructions

1. **Preheat the Oven:**
   - Preheat your oven to 350°F (175°C) and line a baking sheet with parchment paper.
2. **Mix the Dry Ingredients:**
   - In a bowl, combine oats, almond flour, baking soda, cinnamon, and salt.
3. **Mix the Wet Ingredients:**
   - In another bowl, whisk together coconut oil, maple syrup, egg, and vanilla extract.
4. **Combine and Add Raisins:**
   - Add the wet ingredients to the dry ingredients and stir until combined. Fold in raisins.
5. **Shape the Cookies:**
   - Scoop spoonfuls of dough and roll into balls, then place on the baking sheet.
6. **Bake:**
   - Bake for 10-12 minutes, or until the edges are golden. Allow to cool before serving.

Frozen Yogurt Bark with Fruit

Ingredients

- 2 cups plain Greek yogurt
- 2 tbsp honey or maple syrup
- 1/2 tsp vanilla extract
- 1/2 cup mixed berries (strawberries, blueberries, raspberries)
- 1/4 cup sliced almonds or other nuts (optional)

Instructions

1. **Prepare the Yogurt Mixture:**
   - In a bowl, mix the Greek yogurt, honey, and vanilla extract until smooth.
2. **Spread the Yogurt:**
   - Spread the yogurt mixture evenly onto a baking sheet lined with parchment paper.
3. **Top with Fruit and Nuts:**
   - Top the yogurt with mixed berries and sliced almonds.
4. **Freeze:**
   - Place the baking sheet in the freezer for at least 2 hours, or until the yogurt is firm.
5. **Break and Serve:**
   - Once frozen, break the bark into pieces and serve.

Dark Chocolate-Covered Strawberries

Ingredients

- 1 cup dark chocolate chips (70% cocoa or higher)
- 1 tbsp coconut oil
- 12 large strawberries, washed and dried

Instructions

1. **Melt the Chocolate:**
    - In a microwave-safe bowl, melt the dark chocolate chips and coconut oil in 20-second intervals, stirring in between, until smooth.
2. **Dip the Strawberries:**
    - Holding the strawberries by the stem, dip them into the melted chocolate, covering them halfway.
3. **Chill:**
    - Place the chocolate-covered strawberries on a parchment-lined tray and refrigerate for 30 minutes or until the chocolate has set.
4. **Serve:**
    - Enjoy immediately or store in the fridge for up to 3 days.

Paleo Pumpkin Pie

Ingredients

- 1 1/2 cups pumpkin puree
- 1/4 cup coconut milk
- 2 large eggs
- 1/4 cup maple syrup
- 1 tsp cinnamon
- 1/2 tsp ginger
- 1/4 tsp nutmeg
- 1/4 tsp salt
- 1 1/2 cups almond flour (for crust)
- 2 tbsp coconut oil, melted
- 2 tbsp maple syrup (for crust)

Instructions

1. **Prepare the Crust:**
   - Preheat your oven to 350°F (175°C). In a bowl, combine almond flour, melted coconut oil, and maple syrup. Press the mixture into the bottom of a pie dish.
2. **Bake the Crust:**
   - Bake the crust for 10-12 minutes, or until slightly golden. Remove from the oven and set aside.
3. **Prepare the Filling:**
   - In a bowl, whisk together pumpkin puree, coconut milk, eggs, maple syrup, cinnamon, ginger, nutmeg, and salt.
4. **Assemble the Pie:**
   - Pour the pumpkin filling into the pre-baked crust and smooth the top.
5. **Bake:**
   - Bake for 40-45 minutes, or until the center is set and a knife inserted comes out clean.
6. **Cool and Serve:**
   - Let the pie cool completely before serving.

Healthy Lemon Bars

Ingredients

For the crust:

- 1 1/2 cups almond flour
- 1/4 cup melted coconut oil
- 2 tbsp honey or maple syrup
- 1/4 tsp vanilla extract

For the filling:

- 2/3 cup fresh lemon juice (about 3 lemons)
- 2 large eggs
- 1/4 cup honey or maple syrup
- 1/4 tsp vanilla extract
- 1/4 cup coconut flour

Instructions

1. **Prepare the Crust:**
    - Preheat your oven to 350°F (175°C). In a bowl, combine almond flour, melted coconut oil, honey, and vanilla extract. Press the mixture into the bottom of a greased 9x9-inch baking dish.
2. **Bake the Crust:**
    - Bake the crust for 10-12 minutes, or until golden.
3. **Prepare the Filling:**
    - In a bowl, whisk together lemon juice, eggs, honey, vanilla extract, and coconut flour until smooth.
4. **Assemble the Bars:**
    - Pour the filling over the baked crust and smooth the top.
5. **Bake:**
    - Bake for an additional 20-25 minutes, or until the filling is set.
6. **Cool and Serve:**
    - Let the bars cool completely before cutting into squares and serving.

Blueberry Almond Muffins

Ingredients

- 2 cups almond flour
- 1/2 tsp baking soda
- 1/4 tsp salt
- 2 large eggs
- 1/4 cup maple syrup
- 1/4 cup almond milk
- 1 tsp vanilla extract
- 1/2 cup fresh blueberries
- 1/4 cup sliced almonds

Instructions

1. **Preheat the Oven:**
   - Preheat your oven to 350°F (175°C) and line a muffin tin with paper liners.
2. **Mix the Dry Ingredients:**
   - In a bowl, combine almond flour, baking soda, and salt.
3. **Mix the Wet Ingredients:**
   - In another bowl, whisk together eggs, maple syrup, almond milk, and vanilla extract.
4. **Combine and Add Blueberries:**
   - Add the wet ingredients to the dry ingredients and mix until smooth. Gently fold in the blueberries.
5. **Bake:**
   - Spoon the batter into the muffin tin and sprinkle sliced almonds on top. Bake for 18-20 minutes, or until a toothpick comes out clean.
6. **Serve:**
   - Allow the muffins to cool before serving.

Choco-Peanut Butter Smoothie

Ingredients

- 1 banana
- 1 tbsp peanut butter
- 1 tbsp cocoa powder
- 1/2 cup almond milk
- 1/2 cup Greek yogurt
- 1 tsp honey or maple syrup (optional)
- Ice cubes (optional)

Instructions

1. **Blend the Ingredients:**
    - In a blender, combine banana, peanut butter, cocoa powder, almond milk, Greek yogurt, and honey (if using).
2. **Blend Until Smooth:**
    - Blend until smooth, adding ice cubes for a colder smoothie.
3. **Serve:**
    - Pour the smoothie into a glass and enjoy!

Coconut Chia Energy Bites

Ingredients

- 1 cup rolled oats
- 1/2 cup unsweetened shredded coconut
- 2 tbsp chia seeds
- 1/4 cup almond butter
- 1/4 cup honey or maple syrup
- 1 tsp vanilla extract
- Pinch of salt

Instructions

1. **Mix the Ingredients:**
    - In a bowl, combine oats, shredded coconut, chia seeds, almond butter, honey, vanilla extract, and a pinch of salt.
2. **Form the Energy Bites:**
    - Stir until everything is well combined. Roll the mixture into small balls (about 1 inch in diameter).
3. **Chill:**
    - Place the energy bites on a parchment-lined baking sheet and refrigerate for at least 30 minutes to set.
4. **Serve:**
    - Once chilled, enjoy! Store leftovers in an airtight container in the fridge for up to 1 week.

Vegan Chocolate Chip Cookies

Ingredients

- 1 1/2 cups almond flour
- 1/2 tsp baking soda
- 1/4 tsp salt
- 1/4 cup coconut oil, melted
- 1/4 cup maple syrup
- 1 tsp vanilla extract
- 1/2 cup dairy-free chocolate chips

Instructions

1. **Preheat the Oven:**
   - Preheat your oven to 350°F (175°C) and line a baking sheet with parchment paper.
2. **Mix the Dry Ingredients:**
   - In a bowl, combine almond flour, baking soda, and salt.
3. **Mix the Wet Ingredients:**
   - In another bowl, whisk together melted coconut oil, maple syrup, and vanilla extract.
4. **Combine and Add Chocolate Chips:**
   - Add the wet ingredients to the dry ingredients and mix until combined. Fold in the chocolate chips.
5. **Shape the Cookies:**
   - Scoop spoonfuls of dough and roll into balls, then flatten slightly on the baking sheet.
6. **Bake:**
   - Bake for 8-10 minutes, or until the edges are golden.
7. **Cool and Serve:**
   - Allow the cookies to cool on the baking sheet for a few minutes before transferring them to a wire rack.

Caramelized Pineapple with Cinnamon

Ingredients

- 1 ripe pineapple, peeled and sliced
- 1 tbsp coconut oil
- 2 tbsp honey or maple syrup
- 1/2 tsp ground cinnamon
- Pinch of salt

Instructions

1. **Heat the Pan:**
   - In a large skillet, heat coconut oil over medium heat.
2. **Caramelize the Pineapple:**
   - Add the pineapple slices to the pan and cook for about 3-4 minutes on each side, or until golden brown and caramelized.
3. **Add Flavor:**
   - Drizzle honey or maple syrup over the pineapple and sprinkle with cinnamon and a pinch of salt.
4. **Serve:**
   - Serve the caramelized pineapple warm as a sweet treat or dessert.

Baked Oatmeal Cups with Berries

Ingredients

- 2 cups rolled oats
- 1 1/2 cups almond milk
- 1/4 cup maple syrup
- 1 tsp vanilla extract
- 1/2 tsp cinnamon
- 1/2 tsp baking powder
- 1/4 tsp salt
- 1 cup mixed berries (blueberries, raspberries, or strawberries)

Instructions

1. **Preheat the Oven:**
    - Preheat your oven to 350°F (175°C) and grease a muffin tin.
2. **Mix the Ingredients:**
    - In a bowl, combine oats, almond milk, maple syrup, vanilla extract, cinnamon, baking powder, and salt.
3. **Add Berries:**
    - Gently fold in the mixed berries.
4. **Bake:**
    - Divide the oatmeal mixture evenly among the muffin cups. Bake for 20-25 minutes, or until golden and firm.
5. **Serve:**
    - Let the oatmeal cups cool slightly before serving.

Healthy Cheesecake Bites

Ingredients

- 1 1/2 cups raw cashews, soaked for 2 hours
- 1/4 cup coconut milk
- 1/4 cup maple syrup
- 1 tsp vanilla extract
- 1/4 cup coconut oil, melted
- 1/2 cup fresh berries (for topping)

Instructions

1. **Blend the Ingredients:**
    - In a blender or food processor, blend the soaked cashews, coconut milk, maple syrup, vanilla extract, and melted coconut oil until smooth and creamy.
2. **Shape the Bites:**
    - Scoop the mixture into small muffin tin liners or silicone molds and press firmly to shape into bites.
3. **Chill:**
    - Refrigerate the cheesecake bites for at least 3 hours, or until set.
4. **Top and Serve:**
    - Top with fresh berries and serve chilled.

Sweet Potato Brownies

Ingredients

- 1 cup mashed sweet potato (about 1 medium)
- 1/2 cup almond flour
- 1/4 cup cocoa powder
- 1/4 cup maple syrup
- 2 large eggs
- 1/4 cup coconut oil, melted
- 1 tsp vanilla extract
- 1/4 tsp baking soda
- Pinch of salt

Instructions

1. **Preheat the Oven:**
    - Preheat your oven to 350°F (175°C) and line a baking dish with parchment paper.
2. **Mix the Wet Ingredients:**
    - In a bowl, whisk together mashed sweet potato, eggs, maple syrup, melted coconut oil, and vanilla extract.
3. **Combine the Dry Ingredients:**
    - In another bowl, combine almond flour, cocoa powder, baking soda, and salt.
4. **Combine and Bake:**
    - Add the dry ingredients to the wet ingredients and stir until combined. Pour the batter into the prepared baking dish and smooth the top.
5. **Bake:**
    - Bake for 20-25 minutes, or until a toothpick inserted into the center comes out clean.
6. **Serve:**
    - Allow the brownies to cool before slicing and serving.

Coconut Milk Panna Cotta

Ingredients

- 2 cups coconut milk (full-fat)
- 1/4 cup maple syrup
- 1 tsp vanilla extract
- 1 tbsp agar-agar powder (or gelatin if not vegan)
- Fresh berries or fruit for topping

Instructions

1. **Heat the Coconut Milk:**
    - In a saucepan, heat the coconut milk, maple syrup, and vanilla extract over medium heat until it begins to simmer.
2. **Add the Agar-Agar:**
    - Sprinkle in the agar-agar powder and whisk constantly until fully dissolved (about 2-3 minutes). If using gelatin, dissolve it in a bit of water before adding.
3. **Pour and Chill:**
    - Pour the mixture into ramekins or small molds and let it cool. Refrigerate for 3-4 hours, or until set.
4. **Serve:**
    - Once set, top with fresh berries or fruit before serving.

Strawberry Almond Cake

Ingredients

- 2 cups almond flour
- 1/2 cup coconut flour
- 1/4 tsp baking soda
- 1/4 tsp salt
- 3 large eggs
- 1/4 cup honey or maple syrup
- 1/4 cup coconut oil, melted
- 1 tsp vanilla extract
- 1/2 cup chopped fresh strawberries
- 1/4 cup sliced almonds

Instructions

1. **Preheat the Oven:**
   - Preheat your oven to 350°F (175°C) and grease a 9-inch round cake pan.
2. **Mix the Dry Ingredients:**
   - In a bowl, combine almond flour, coconut flour, baking soda, and salt.
3. **Mix the Wet Ingredients:**
   - In another bowl, whisk together eggs, honey or maple syrup, melted coconut oil, and vanilla extract.
4. **Combine the Batter:**
   - Add the wet ingredients to the dry ingredients and mix until smooth. Fold in the chopped strawberries.
5. **Bake:**
   - Pour the batter into the prepared cake pan and sprinkle sliced almonds on top. Bake for 25-30 minutes, or until golden brown.
6. **Cool and Serve:**
   - Let the cake cool before slicing and serving.

Matcha Energy Bars

Ingredients

- 1 cup rolled oats
- 1/2 cup almond butter
- 1/4 cup maple syrup
- 1 tbsp matcha powder
- 1/4 cup chia seeds
- 1/4 cup shredded coconut
- 1/4 tsp vanilla extract
- Pinch of salt

Instructions

1. **Prepare the Mixture:**
    - In a bowl, combine oats, almond butter, maple syrup, matcha powder, chia seeds, shredded coconut, vanilla extract, and salt.
2. **Press into a Pan:**
    - Press the mixture into a lined 8x8-inch baking dish, spreading it evenly.
3. **Chill and Slice:**
    - Refrigerate for 1-2 hours until firm. Cut into bars and store in an airtight container.

Maple Cinnamon Roasted Nuts

Ingredients

- 2 cups mixed nuts (almonds, walnuts, cashews)
- 2 tbsp maple syrup
- 1 tsp cinnamon
- Pinch of salt

Instructions

1. **Preheat the Oven:**
   - Preheat the oven to 350°F (175°C) and line a baking sheet with parchment paper.
2. **Mix the Nuts:**
   - In a bowl, toss the nuts with maple syrup, cinnamon, and salt.
3. **Roast:**
   - Spread the nuts in a single layer on the baking sheet and roast for 15-20 minutes, stirring halfway through.
4. **Cool and Serve:**
   - Let the nuts cool completely before serving or storing in an airtight container.

Date-Sweetened Brownies

Ingredients

- 1 1/2 cups dates, pitted and soaked
- 1/2 cup almond flour
- 1/4 cup cocoa powder
- 1/4 tsp baking soda
- 1/4 tsp salt
- 1/4 cup almond butter
- 1 tsp vanilla extract
- 2 large eggs

Instructions

1. **Preheat the Oven:**
    - Preheat the oven to 350°F (175°C) and grease a small baking pan.
2. **Prepare the Date Mixture:**
    - Blend the soaked dates in a food processor until smooth. Add almond butter, eggs, and vanilla extract, blending until combined.
3. **Mix Dry Ingredients:**
    - In a separate bowl, combine almond flour, cocoa powder, baking soda, and salt.
4. **Combine and Bake:**
    - Add the dry ingredients to the wet mixture and mix. Pour into the baking pan and bake for 20-25 minutes.
5. **Cool and Serve:**
    - Let cool before slicing and serving.

Apple Almond Crumble

Ingredients

- 4 medium apples, peeled and sliced
- 1/2 cup almond flour
- 1/4 cup rolled oats
- 1/4 cup chopped almonds
- 2 tbsp coconut oil, melted
- 2 tbsp maple syrup
- 1 tsp cinnamon
- Pinch of salt

Instructions

1. **Preheat the Oven:**
   - Preheat the oven to 350°F (175°C) and grease a baking dish.
2. **Prepare the Apples:**
   - Arrange the apple slices in the baking dish. Sprinkle with a little cinnamon.
3. **Make the Crumble Topping:**
   - In a bowl, mix almond flour, oats, chopped almonds, melted coconut oil, maple syrup, cinnamon, and salt.
4. **Top and Bake:**
   - Spread the crumble mixture over the apples and bake for 25-30 minutes, or until golden and bubbling.
5. **Serve:**
   - Let cool slightly before serving.

Healthy Chocolate Coconut Cupcakes

Ingredients

- 1 cup almond flour
- 1/4 cup cocoa powder
- 1/4 tsp baking soda
- 1/4 tsp salt
- 2 large eggs
- 1/4 cup maple syrup
- 1/4 cup coconut oil, melted
- 1 tsp vanilla extract
- 1/4 cup shredded coconut

Instructions

1. **Preheat the Oven:**
   - Preheat the oven to 350°F (175°C) and line a muffin tin with paper liners.
2. **Mix the Dry Ingredients:**
   - In a bowl, combine almond flour, cocoa powder, baking soda, and salt.
3. **Mix the Wet Ingredients:**
   - In another bowl, whisk together eggs, maple syrup, melted coconut oil, and vanilla extract.
4. **Combine the Mixtures:**
   - Add the wet ingredients to the dry and mix until smooth.
5. **Fill and Bake:**
   - Spoon the batter into the muffin tin and sprinkle with shredded coconut. Bake for 18-20 minutes.
6. **Cool and Serve:**
   - Let cool before serving.

Chia Jam on Almond Crackers

Ingredients

- 1/2 cup fresh or frozen berries
- 1 tbsp maple syrup
- 1 tbsp chia seeds
- 10 almond crackers

Instructions

1. **Make the Jam:**
    - In a saucepan, cook the berries with maple syrup over medium heat for 5-7 minutes. Mash the berries, and then stir in chia seeds. Cook for another 2-3 minutes until thickened.
2. **Serve:**
    - Spoon the chia jam onto almond crackers and serve immediately.

Vegan Lemon Coconut Truffles

Ingredients

- 1 cup shredded coconut
- 1/4 cup coconut oil, melted
- 1/4 cup maple syrup
- Zest of 1 lemon
- 1 tbsp lemon juice
- Pinch of salt

Instructions

1. **Mix the Ingredients:**
    - In a bowl, combine shredded coconut, coconut oil, maple syrup, lemon zest, lemon juice, and salt.
2. **Form the Truffles:**
    - Roll the mixture into small balls and place on a parchment-lined tray.
3. **Chill and Serve:**
    - Refrigerate for 1-2 hours until firm.

Banana Chia Pudding

Ingredients

- 1 ripe banana, mashed
- 1 cup almond milk
- 2 tbsp chia seeds
- 1 tbsp maple syrup
- 1/2 tsp vanilla extract

Instructions

1. **Mix the Ingredients:**
    - In a bowl, combine the mashed banana, almond milk, chia seeds, maple syrup, and vanilla extract.
2. **Refrigerate:**
    - Stir well, cover, and refrigerate for at least 4 hours or overnight.
3. **Serve:**
    - Top with fresh fruit before serving.

Almond Butter Banana Ice Cream

Ingredients

- 2 ripe bananas, frozen and sliced
- 2 tbsp almond butter
- 1/2 tsp vanilla extract
- Pinch of salt

Instructions

1. **Blend the Ingredients:**
   - In a food processor, blend the frozen banana slices, almond butter, vanilla extract, and salt until smooth.
2. **Serve:**
   - Scoop into bowls and serve immediately, or freeze for later.

Avocado Lime Cheesecake

Ingredients

- 2 ripe avocados, peeled and pitted
- 1/2 cup lime juice
- 1/4 cup honey or maple syrup
- 1 cup raw cashews (soaked for 4-6 hours)
- 1/4 cup coconut oil, melted
- 1 tsp vanilla extract
- Pinch of salt
- 1 cup almond flour (for crust)
- 1/4 cup shredded coconut (for crust)
- 2 tbsp coconut oil (for crust)

Instructions

1. **Prepare the Crust:**
    - Preheat the oven to 350°F (175°C). In a food processor, blend almond flour, shredded coconut, and coconut oil until combined. Press the mixture into the bottom of a pie dish and bake for 10 minutes. Let cool.
2. **Make the Cheesecake Filling:**
    - In a blender, combine avocados, lime juice, honey, soaked cashews, coconut oil, vanilla extract, and a pinch of salt. Blend until smooth and creamy.
3. **Assemble and Chill:**
    - Pour the avocado-lime filling over the cooled crust. Chill in the refrigerator for at least 4 hours, or overnight, until firm.
4. **Serve:**
    - Slice and enjoy!

Chocolate-Peanut Butter Protein Balls

Ingredients

- 1/2 cup natural peanut butter
- 1/4 cup cocoa powder
- 1/4 cup honey or maple syrup
- 1/2 cup protein powder (chocolate or vanilla)
- 1/4 cup oats
- Pinch of salt

Instructions

1. **Mix the Ingredients:**
   - In a bowl, combine peanut butter, cocoa powder, honey, protein powder, oats, and salt. Stir until everything is well combined.
2. **Form the Balls:**
   - Roll the mixture into bite-sized balls (about 1 inch in diameter).
3. **Chill and Serve:**
   - Place the balls on a tray and refrigerate for at least 30 minutes before serving.

Pumpkin Energy Bars

Ingredients

- 1 cup rolled oats
- 1/2 cup canned pumpkin puree
- 1/4 cup almond butter
- 1/4 cup maple syrup
- 1 tsp pumpkin pie spice
- 1/4 cup ground flaxseeds
- 1/4 cup chocolate chips (optional)

Instructions

1. **Mix the Ingredients:**
    - In a bowl, combine oats, pumpkin puree, almond butter, maple syrup, pumpkin pie spice, and ground flaxseeds. Stir until well combined.
2. **Press into a Pan:**
    - Press the mixture into a lined 8x8-inch pan, spreading it evenly.
3. **Refrigerate and Slice:**
    - Refrigerate for 1-2 hours until firm, then slice into bars.

Raw Chocolate Coconut Fudge

Ingredients

- 1 cup shredded coconut
- 1/2 cup coconut oil, melted
- 1/4 cup cocoa powder
- 1/4 cup maple syrup or honey
- 1 tsp vanilla extract
- Pinch of salt

Instructions

1. **Mix the Ingredients:**
    - In a bowl, combine melted coconut oil, cocoa powder, maple syrup, vanilla extract, and salt. Stir in the shredded coconut until fully combined.
2. **Set the Fudge:**
    - Pour the mixture into a lined baking dish and spread evenly. Refrigerate for 2-3 hours until firm.
3. **Slice and Serve:**
    - Once set, slice into squares and serve.

Oat and Honey Granola Bars

Ingredients

- 2 cups rolled oats
- 1/4 cup honey or maple syrup
- 1/4 cup almond butter
- 1/4 cup dried fruit (raisins, cranberries, etc.)
- 1/4 cup nuts or seeds (optional)
- 1 tsp vanilla extract
- Pinch of salt

Instructions

1. **Preheat the Oven:**
   - Preheat the oven to 350°F (175°C). Line a baking dish with parchment paper.
2. **Mix the Ingredients:**
   - In a bowl, combine oats, honey, almond butter, dried fruit, nuts or seeds, vanilla extract, and salt. Stir to combine.
3. **Bake:**
   - Press the mixture into the prepared baking dish and bake for 12-15 minutes, or until golden brown.
4. **Cool and Slice:**
   - Let the granola bars cool before slicing into bars.

Strawberry Coconut Sorbet

Ingredients

- 2 cups fresh or frozen strawberries
- 1/4 cup coconut milk
- 2 tbsp maple syrup or honey
- 1 tsp lemon juice

Instructions

1. **Blend the Ingredients:**
    - In a blender, combine strawberries, coconut milk, maple syrup, and lemon juice. Blend until smooth.
2. **Freeze:**
    - Pour the mixture into a shallow container and freeze for 3-4 hours, stirring every 30 minutes to break up ice crystals.
3. **Serve:**
    - Once the sorbet has set, scoop and serve!

Cinnamon Pecan Bites

Ingredients

- 1 cup pecans
- 1/4 cup dates, pitted
- 1 tbsp maple syrup
- 1/2 tsp cinnamon
- Pinch of salt

Instructions

1. **Blend the Ingredients:**
    - In a food processor, blend pecans, dates, maple syrup, cinnamon, and salt until combined and sticky.
2. **Form the Bites:**
    - Roll the mixture into small bite-sized balls.
3. **Chill and Serve:**
    - Refrigerate for at least 30 minutes before serving.

Mango-Coconut Popsicles

Ingredients

- 2 cups fresh mango, chopped
- 1/2 cup coconut milk
- 2 tbsp honey or maple syrup

Instructions

1. **Blend the Ingredients:**
    - In a blender, blend mango, coconut milk, and honey until smooth.
2. **Freeze:**
    - Pour the mixture into popsicle molds and freeze for 4-6 hours.
3. **Serve:**
    - Once frozen, remove from molds and enjoy!

Almond Flour Chocolate Cake

Ingredients

- 2 cups almond flour
- 1/2 cup cocoa powder
- 1/2 tsp baking soda
- 1/4 tsp salt
- 4 large eggs
- 1/2 cup maple syrup
- 1/2 cup coconut oil, melted
- 1 tsp vanilla extract

Instructions

1. **Preheat the Oven:**
    - Preheat the oven to 350°F (175°C). Grease and line a round cake pan.
2. **Mix Dry Ingredients:**
    - In a bowl, combine almond flour, cocoa powder, baking soda, and salt.
3. **Mix Wet Ingredients:**
    - In another bowl, whisk together eggs, maple syrup, melted coconut oil, and vanilla extract.
4. **Combine and Bake:**
    - Add the dry ingredients to the wet ingredients and stir until smooth. Pour into the cake pan and bake for 25-30 minutes, or until a toothpick comes out clean.
5. **Cool and Serve:**
    - Let cool before serving.